WHITE BLIGHT

ATHENA   FARROKHZAD

WHITE BLIGHT

TRANSLATED BY
JENNIFER HAYASHIDA

ARGOS BOOKS

Portions of this work have appeared previously in: AFRICAN AND BLACK
DIASPORAS: AN INTERNATIONAL JOURNAL (Eds. Lena Sawyer and Ylva Habel),
PEN AMERICA: A JOURNAL FOR WRITERS AND READERS, TIDSKRIFTEN FUL, and
TWO LINES PRESS.

ISBN 978-1-938247-21-7

Library of Congress Control Number: 2015949326

Original title in Swedish — Vitsvit

The translation of this book was supported
by grants from the Swedish Arts Council
and the PEN/Heim Translation Fund

Argos Books
www.argosbooks.org

My family arrived here in a Marxist tradition

My mother immediately filled the house with Santa knick-knacks
Weighed the pros and cons of the plastic Christmas tree
as if the problem were hers

During the day she distinguished between long and short vowels
as if the sounds that came out of her mouth
could wash the olive oil from her skin

My mother let bleach run through her syntax
On the other side of punctuation her syllables became whiter
than a winter in Norrland

My mother built us a future consisting of quantity of life
In the suburban basement she lined up canned goods
as if preparing for a war

In the evenings she searched for recipes and peeled potatoes
as if it were her history inscribed
in the Jansson's temptation casserole

To think that I sucked at those breasts
To think that she put her barbarism in my mouth

My mother said: It seems it has never occurred to you that it is from your name

civilization descends

My mother said: The darkness in my belly is the only darkness you command

My mother said: You are a dreamer born to turn straight eyes aslant

My mother said: If you could regard the circumstances as extenuating

you would let me off easier

My mother said: Never underestimate the trouble people will take

to formulate truths possible for them to bear

My mother said: You were not fit to live even from the start

My mother said: A woman dug out her mother's eyes with her fingers

so the mother would be spared the sight of the daughter's decline

My father said: You have a tendency towards metaphysics

Still I schooled you in the means of production

when your milk teeth were intact

My mother said: Your father lived for the day of judgement

So did your mother, but she was forced to other ambitions

12

My mother said: In your father's sleep you are executed together

In your father's dream you form a geneology of revolutionaries

My father said: Your mother fed you with imported silver spoons

Your mother was everywhere in your face

frantically combed out the curls

My mother said: For a lifetime I envied your father's traumas

until I realized that my own were far more remarkable

My mother said: I have spent a fortune on your piano lessons

But at my funeral you will refuse to play

My mother took the dream out of my father's hand and said:

All this sugar will not make you sweeter

Walk a lap around the house before you take the insulin

My father said: I have lived my life, I have lived my life

I have done my share

Now nothing remains of the halcyon days of youth

My mother said to my brother: Beware of strangers

Remember that you have nothing to return to

should they become dangerous

My brother said: I had such a strange dream

That dawn died in my eyes before sleep had cleared

A humanity of sugar and slaughter

When I bid farewell to the light I knew everything

My mother said: From the division of cells

from a genetic material

from your father's head

But not from me

My father said: From the clash of civilizations

from a fundamental antagonism

from my tired head

But not from her

My father said: If it were possible to compete in martyrdom

your mother would do everything to lose

My mother said: The heart is not like the knee that can be bent at will

My father said: Even the rooster who does not crow gets to see the sun rise

My mother said: But if the hen does not lay an egg she will be served for dinner

My father said: Your brother shaved before his beard started to grow

Your brother saw the terrorist's face in the mirror

and wanted a flat iron for Christmas

My brother said: Some day I want to die in a country

where people can pronounce my name

My brother said: Do not think it is in your power to offer me anything

My father said: Whose father are you rendering

My mother said: Whose mother are you rendering

My brother said: Whose brother is being referred to

My grandmother said: If you don't finish chopping the vegetables soon

there won't be any dinner

21

My father said: To those who have more will be given

and from those who lack even more will be taken

My mother said: Take some more milk before it turns

My mother said: Wouldn't it be strange to feel

a single night like this one

my language in your mouth

My father said: One spoonful for the executioners

one spoonful for the emancipators

one spoonful for the hungry masses

And one spoonful for me

My mother handed the glass to her mother and said: Now we are even

Here is the milk back

My grandmother said: Your mother descends from the rising sun

She was named after the flower bud since she was born in spring

Your mother named you after a warrior to prepare you for winter

My grandmother said: During spring in Marghacho mint grew along the streams

Does the poem you are writing reveal any of this

My grandmother said: You snot-nosed little mutt

Come here and I'll take your measurements and knit you a wool sweater

My mother said: If we meet again we will not let on that we knew each other

when you were hungry and it was I who carried the milk

My brother said: Black milk of dawn, we drink you at night

The past is an assault never to be completed

My mother said: Write like this

For my opportunities my mother sacrificed everything

I must be worthy of her

everything I write will be true

My grandmother said: Write like this

Mothers and languages resemble each other

in that they incessantly lie about everything

My mother said: All families have their stories

but for them to emerge requires someone

with a particular will to disfigure

My mother said: You distort the injury with your unfortunate lie

There is a muteness that cannot be translated

My brother said: There is always something imperfect that remains inescapable

There is always something incomplete missing

My mother said: Your family will never recover from the lie that binds

My father said: Your family will never return to the rooftops when it cools down

My brother said: Your family will never be resurrected like roses after a fire

My grandmother said: There is a time for everything under the sun

time to return to the rooftops when it cools down

My grandmother said: Pistachios for the toothless

rosaries for the godless

rugs for the homeless

and a mother for you

My father said: Jobs for the jobless

wages for the wageless

papers for the paperless

and a father for you

My brother said: Cables for the wireless

organs for the bodyless

transfusions for the heartless

and a brother for you

My mother said: Oxygen for the lifeless

vitamins for the listless

prostheses for the limbless

and a language for you

My mother said: I will reclaim what belongs to me

You will meet death robbed of language

Speechless you came, speechless you will return

My father said: I wrote of bread and justice

and as long as the starving could read

the font did not matter to me

My father said: The serif pricks my fingers

My father said: How much resistance can human fat bear

before the lashes of the whip become permanent

My father said: If you forget the alphabet

you will find it on my back

My father said: Only when you forgive the one who has turned you in

will you know the meaning of violence

My father said: There were those who were executed at dawn before sleep had cleared

My mother said: There were those who had to pay for the bullets

to bury their daughters

My mother said: Into what victor's night did this victory throw us

My father said: Your uncle was there on a crackling phone line

Your uncle refined his metaphors with every lash of the whip

My brother said: Do not bury me here

Bury me where the lashes of the whip are virtual

My uncle said: You will forget everything

except memory, which you will always remember

I remember that before the war the soldier chewed with my teeth

The agitator screamed with my throat

My uncle said: For my sloping shoulders

for my constant smile

For this pile of rocks that was once my house

My uncle said: Is there a puddle where war has not washed its bloody hands

My uncle said: There were those who were executed at every sunrise

There were those who remained and saw the sentences carried out

My mother said: Why do they invoke god from the rooftops

Have they forgotten that it was god who held the whip

when their mothers were tortured

My mother said: Show me someone who inhabits their face

and I will show you the one who no face deserves

My brother said: I want to know who was humiliated for my sake

What affinities I am guilty of

and what reprisals await

My brother said: There is a slaughter that will always go on

for a sign no one can remember

My uncle said: What will become of us when we have fought for our emancipation

with the same means that imprisoned us

My father said: Bodies without clarity, bodies without shadow

My brother said: The habit of kneeling will be replaced by the joy of commanding

My father said: There is a war that takes place in the guts

There is an enemy who rushes forth from my hands and lips

My brother said: There is a fever that escalates with every blow

There is a machine that hammers when turned off

My father said: Violence is a language in which the hand excels

My father said: When we give according to ability and receive according to need

My mother said: When we give according to ability and receive according to need

My brother said: When all injustices and history itself ends

My grandmother said: When you are as old as I am

Then all injustices and history itself will end

My father said: Do not bury me here

Bury me where all property has been expropriated

Do not give me a tombstone, dedicate your halcyon days to me

My mother said: It is better to dream that you are dead

than to die of all the dreams that invent you

My grandmother said: Do not bury me here

Bury me where the mint grows along the streams

Set the table for a feast, serve my most delicious stew

My uncle said: The war has never ceased

You have only ceased being the victim of war

My mother said: Do not bury me here

Bury me where the veneer of civilization has peeled

Spit out my language, return the milk to me

My grandmother said: When you are from a place it is inescapable

You can say I changed there

I left the gathering of stones

Or I was never intended for frost-ridden dawn

But you cannot say I am from nowhere

I belong to no place

My father said: The one who travels is redundant to the place they came from

My mother said: The one who travels thinks they are essential to the place they come to

My father said: The one who travels is redundant to the place they come to

My mother said: The one who travels thinks they were essential to the place they came from

My uncle said: The one who travels knows nothing about place

My father said: We are still there, even if time has separated us from the place

My mother said: Our ceilings are as high as the floors warrant

My father said: The farther you move from the scene of the crime,

the more you are bound to it

My mother said: The more you care for the wound,

the more it festers

My grandmother said: What you lose on the swings you gain on the roundabouts

My uncle said: Do not forget that you walked these streets as a child

Do not forget that all that matters in a revolution

is the daughters' decisions between the lines of the poem

My mother said: If you do not speak to someone for whom you can abandon language

there is no point in speaking

My uncle said: If you do not tremble when you cross a border

it is not the border you have crossed

My grandmother said: When you sit up in the saddle you should grip the reins tightly

But when they saddle you up

then you should gallop

My grandmother said: Belonging is like a mirror

If it breaks you can repair it

My mother said: But in the reflection a shard is missing

My father said: Since no one who belongs to you is buried in this earth

this earth does not belong to you

My mother said: Only when you bury me in this earth

will this earth belong to you

My mother said: Like a mummy's bandages you bind up the story

Like a river where the dirty waters of history run

My mother said: Time will catch up with your tongue

My father said: Everything you write will be used against you

My mother said: In due time everything will be turned against you

My mother said: You go through everything in search of something to disfigure

My mother said: Only the line that provokes my tears

do you consider worthy of notation

My mother said: You build the poem from my shortcomings

Then you say the poem is not mine to mourn

My mother said: It is about you your throat remains silent

My father said: It is about you your silence speaks

My mother said: You will speak of what you do not understand

and have no strength for

and it is not you

and not your ground

My father said: Who is speechless in a poem about language

My grandmother said: Who is bared in a poem about desire

My mother said: Who is betrayed in a poem about betrayal

My brother said: The price is never as high as when you think no one will pay

My father said: Show me someone who has abandoned their language

and I will show you the one who no language contains

My brother said: We are nothing but the sum of the harm inflicted on us by language

The sum of the harm we inflict

My father said: Speak the language that pays for your bread

My grandmother said: Speak the language that keeps its distance

from what has taken place in words

My brother said: Speak the language that gives life to the machine

My mother said: Speak the language worth the price of betraying me

My father said: You are the spitting image of your mother

You are everything your mother despises

My father said: Also in the eyes of the cockroach

its own child is the most beautiful

My mother said: I will remove infectious vermin

Darkness from humanity

My mother said: There is a barbarism that never melts into air

60

My father said: When age has overpowered your body it will give itself away

When you have lost all ability only the mother tongue remains

My mother said: If you kill me in this language it is yours to keep

My father said: Write that this language kills you, write in this language

My brother said: You are credible if they recognize you

My father said: If you ever give them the satisfaction

of having their images confirmed

I will wash my hands of you

My mother said: Your difference is immobile and mute

No, your difference is a conjured monster demanding its tribute

Your difference is doomed to repeat its question

My brother said: The only language you have to condemn the crime

is the language of the criminal

and the language of the criminal

is a language invented to justify the crime

My brother said: Like an accomplice among them

like a henchman among them

with fingers alarmingly red

from the blood of their civilization

My brother said: When conceit spoils the gaze

when resentment hardens the heart

when injustices rest around the mouth

Then you will remember one bite through another

My mother said: Say my name as the spittle lands

My brother said: We will persist in laying waste

We will be as sensitive as our most tender points

We are not obligated to beat our heads against walls

We are a grinding movement, we will persevere

My grandmother said: A wound at dawn where the sleepless night forces its way in

A darkness that cannot be grasped

A sensation of heavens where other moons rest

My grandmother said: Where is the wind that will rescue us

My mother said: Where is the milk demanded by each breath

My father: Where are the switches we bound for our backs

My grandmother said: Maybe one day

when the mint blooms along the streams

we will meet and say to each other

we have never tasted a more delicious saffron rice

My mother said: Maybe one day

on the other side of this unfortunate lie

we will meet and formulate a phrase

we thought was reserved only for others

67

My father said: You will articulate my faceless longing

There is a word that is the last to abandon humanity

Tomorrow I am one syllable closer

My father said: Turn me into a stone for your sling

turn my mouth into lips for your lament

my knees to the crumbled pillars of your humiliation

My brother said: Memories thrive on the ground

like a humble weed

How far must we dig in our traces

to overhear the lament of the roots

My grandmother said: You will guard their piercing peal

You will plant it in a ground

that moves at the pace of your restlessness

My brother said: All those seeds sentenced

to fall into this earth and never bloom

It is for them the earth will split

This vital book exposes the dense tectonics churning beneath migrant dreams. Accusatory, loving, full of grief and sage truths, Athena Farrokhzad's WHITE BLIGHT speaks eloquently to the troubled inheritance of diasporic survival. Through a litany of terse voices, Jennifer Hayashida's sensitive translation describes the nexus of filial obligations and projections under which the narrator sinks from view. The intense beauty of devastation and the poignancy of betrayal emerge with startling frankness: "Your family will never be resurrected like roses after a fire." "I have spent a fortune for your piano lessons / But at my funeral you will refuse to play." These white lines make me ask, what has been bleached out in all of our stories? I read this book, and I remembered my humanity.

— Sueyeun Juliette Lee

It is hard to explain not just the resonance of Athena Farrokhzad's work but of Farrokhzad herself. She is a major figure in Sweden, an outspoken feminist and leftist. She is also a stunning writer. On its surface WHITE BLIGHT is a story of migration, how it shapes and misshapes the familiar. Everyone in this poem has something to say about immigration's trauma, on the impact globalization has on all sorts of intimacy, even as they are so rarely talking to each other. It is also a poem that moves through many registers. At moments it is mannered and metaphoric. At other moments frank and colloquial, intimate too. And Jennifer Hayashida has skillfully translated this complicated work into an ease of English.

— Juliana Spahr

In WHITE BLIGHT, Athena Farrokhzad evokes a language of feeling that is vivid and deeply familiar. The poem performs as intimately as memory, but with the direct language of confession or accusation. In this world, the family unit nurtures by prolonging disquietude, as there is no forgetting the ruptures of exile and immigration. Still these voices yearn to be proven wrong in a future they cannot predict. The pith and force of the language shines through in Jennifer Hayashida's careful translation, both polished and knife-sharp.

— Wendy S. Walters